How to Study for Success in Science, Math, and Engineering Courses

▶▶▶

Corrections

On page 26, the units at the bottom of the page should read:

$$\frac{kg * meter / \sec ond^2}{meter^2 / \sec ond^2} = \frac{kg}{meter}$$

On page 60, the quadratic equation should read:

Step 2: $x = \dfrac{-b \pm \sqrt{b^2 - 4ac}}{2a}$ where in this case, a = 3, b = 7, and c = -2.

Step 3: Plug the numbers into the formula to get the final answer:

$$x = \frac{-7 \pm \sqrt{7^2 - (4*3*(-2))}}{2*3} = 0.26 \text{ or } -2.59$$

How to Study for Success in Science, Math, and Engineering Courses

▶▶

Amy E. Bieber, Ph.D.

Sunflower Publishing
New York

CIP Data is available
Publishing in the United States in 2004
by Sunflower Publishing, New York, N.Y. 10001

First Edition

ISBN: 0-9709491-1-1

Printed in the United States
Design and type formatting by Arlene Schleifer Goldberg

2 4 6 8 10 9 7 5 3 1

Contents

▶▶▶▶▶▶▶▶▶▶▶▶▶▶▶▶▶▶▶▶▶▶▶▶▶▶▶▶▶▶▶▶▶▶▶▶▶▶

This book is dedicated to all students
who love to learn.

Thanks to Heidi Sanchez for proofreading
and advice about citation information and
to Gene Sanchez for literally "making" this
book possible.

Chapter 1:

Introduction

▶ ▶

This book is intended for college students (or advanced high school students) of all levels and of all majors who are taking technical courses. This includes science, engineering, and math courses, both introductory and advanced. Whether you are a freshman or senior, it is not too late to learn to succeed in technical courses. Whether you have always had trouble with math and science or you did very well in high school and are now being seriously challenged for the first time in college, this book will have something to offer you. I am a physics professor and have taught courses in lasers and optics, acoustics, general physics, and astronomy. I have a Ph.D in Optics from the University of Rochester Institute of Optics, a Bachelor's Degree in Electrical Engineering from The Johns Hopkins University, an Associate's Degree in Music Electronic Technology from The City University of New York, as well as several years of industrial engineering/science experience. As a student, I had to develop good study methods in order to do well at extremely competitive schools. As a professor, my experience with students at different levels of expertise is diverse. I have worked with engineering and science majors in my specialty courses who have taken several semesters of calculus and who plan to go to graduate school, and I have worked with arts and marketing majors in my astronomy courses who don't have any college-level math skills and not much of an interest in science. I have learned a lot from my experiences as a student and as a professor dealing with a diverse student population. I wrote this book because students are always asking me how they should study for physics courses. Also, I so often see students struggling and making things difficult for themselves because they don't know how to plan ahead and study properly—I wanted to try to help.

Some people take technical courses because it will become part of their career, and some take them because it is a graduation requirement for their major. Some people are extremely enthusiastic about the courses and some go into the courses assuming that they will hate them and it will be impossible to understand it. The study methods and practices described in this book can be beneficial to all of these kinds of students. Having a good attitude and disciplined study methods are the key to success in college; specific methods for dealing with the special issues which arise in technical courses are described in detail in this book.

Chapter 2
Choosing Courses

▶ ▶

Choosing the courses that you will take each semester is something that should be done in consultation with an academic advisor, even if you are fairly sure that you know what you are doing. If you are working from a catalog, which of course you should read before seriously planning your program, talk to an advisor anyway because sometimes the information in the catalog is outdated. Some courses that are listed in the catalog never actually run, and some only run once a year; you won't know which ones do and don't run every semester unless you speak to someone in the department. An academic advisor might have new information about upcoming curriculum changes of which you may not be aware, and they also have the experience to recommend certain courses which should or should not be taken together. You should consult an academic advisor in your major department as soon as you choose a major so that you can plan ahead and make the most of your program. If you have not chosen a major, you should consult an academic advisor in the office of advising and counseling at your school to plan a program that will keep your options open.

Assuming you have chosen a major, your program should seek to fulfill prerequisite and core requirements as early as possible. Make sure you know what these requirements are for your major. Or, if you don't have a specific major but you know the general area you want, like engineering, find out what courses are required for all engineering majors (like several semesters of calculus) and start taking those courses. Also, most schools have early registration periods; it is highly recommended that you register at this time so that you do not get closed out of courses that you want to take.

Your advisor can also help you to choose an appropriate credit load. This is a balancing act between taking enough credits so that you stay on track to graduate on time, yet not overloading yourself so that you become overwhelmed and discouraged. A good rule of thumb, especially for technical courses, is to plan on spending at least one, and more likely two, hours outside of the class for every hour you spend inside the class. I'm not kidding! College is a big commitment in many ways, not the least of which is the demand it makes on your time. Do not try to take more credits than you have time for. Many students make the mistake of thinking that 12 credits will require 12-15 hours a week and that means they can still work 30 hours a week at a job. If you attempt something like this you will not do well in your courses, you will not do well at your job, you'll be tired and stressed all the time, and you'll probably end up withdrawing from at least one course for which you will lose the tuition. Don't expect the professor to make exceptions for you because you didn't allow enough time in your schedule to actually learn the material! Of course, this not only applies to people with jobs and children, but also to those who are double-majoring or trying to graduate a year early. Do not attempt to take on more than you can handle: a twelve to fifteen credit load is equivalent to a full-time job. Treat it with the seriousness it deserves.

If you think you might be interested in transferring to another college at some point, talk to your advisor about which courses are usually transferable and which are not. Also speak to someone at the college to which you wish to transfer to verify the information. Sometimes you can change your schedule so that you still meet your degree requirements while taking courses that are more likely to transfer to other schools, should you decide to go that route. This all requires advance planning; it would be a shame to take an entire program of courses only to find out that they do not transfer to the school you want to go to and that, had you selected different courses, you could have transferred the credit.

If you have not yet chosen a major, keep an open mind and explore everything related to your interests. Talk to faculty members from many different departments; there might be areas of study or career options that you have never heard of that would be right up your alley. Sit in on different types of courses to get a feel for what that area of study is like, and talk to other students in that major. Always get multiple opinions, because you wouldn't want just one person's experience to sway you unduly. It also can be very beneficial to speak to someone already working in the industry you are considering for your career. To find someone to speak to, you can ask a professor in that major department for an industry contact or an alumni working in that field, or you can ask for the same information at the career services office on your campus. Again, try to speak to more than one person, because if someone had a bad experience or decided that the career choice he/she made was a mistake, listen to what this person says about the pitfalls, but it doesn't necessarily mean that the career choice would be a bad one for *you*. Many times there are clubs or organizations on campus that are professionally oriented. For example, there might be an engineering club or a physics club. Go to a few meetings to see what these clubs are about and if the activities interest you. This can be a good way to get more information about careers and to meet people who have chosen that particular career. Use every resource available on your campus to get as much career information as you possibly can.

Chapter 3

Taking Notes and Asking Questions

▶▶▶

Good note-taking is one of the most important skills any college student can have, and yet it is never taught! Most students make the mistake of only writing down what the professor writes on the blackboard. However, most professors do not write down everything that is noteworthy because to do so is very tiring. Therefore, you must learn to extract the most important points from the professor's words. If he or she writes on the board, great, but don't rely on that, and don't discount whatever he or she says that never makes it onto the blackboard. Listen to the professor carefully; he or she will vocally emphasize things that are important even if they don't get written down. Once you get to know the professor's personality and speaking style, it will become easier to pick out the important points in the lecture.

It is difficult to write full sentences while someone is

talking, so try to write keywords that will trigger your memory later, and then you can fill in the blanks and elaborate. Your notes should have structure and should tell a story of what went on in the lecture. Skip lines and make paragraphs. Use underlining, arrows, or any method you like to highlight important points. Put boxes around the most important equations. For example, if a professor does a multi-step derivation of an equation, put a box around the final result. Make sure the notes are coherent so that when you look at them one month later, they will make sense to you. Ideally, they should make sense to someone who missed the lecture and would like to copy your notes, but this is not always possible because of the high speed at which some professors deliver material. After you go through the notes and fix them up, though, someone else should definitely be able to borrow them and follow them.

You should draw diagrams as often as possible to illustrate important points in your notes, even if the professor did not draw a diagram. Bring two different colored pens, or a pencil and a pen, so that you can distinguish between different quantities or directions in a drawing. It is often necessary in technical courses to make three-dimensional drawings; having two different colors can be greatly helpful in achieving this.

Important: After each lecture, go over your notes and make sure they make sense. Fill in details that you did not have time to write down during the class. Do it the same day so you remember the details! Consult the book, a classmate, or the professor if there is anything you can't figure out. Don't leave things in your notes that don't make sense because they will pile up, and when exam time comes you'll have a lot of work to do to backtrack and figure out what the professor was talking about weeks ago. This is elaborated upon in the chapter on studying for exams.

I'll never forget when I was a senior in college and they changed the graduation requirements, causing me to take a freshman-level chemistry course in my senior year. I was sitting behind a freshman student in a large, sloped lecture hall, so it was easy for me to see her notebook. The professor was madly scribbling things all over six different blackboards, and he was starting to run out of room but didn't want to erase anything. He found a little empty spot in the middle of one of the boards and put two squiggly lines on either side of the empty spot so as not to confuse his new writing with what was already on the board. He then wrote something in that space. I just happened to glance down at this girl's notebook at that moment and, to my shock and amusement, she had written down the new piece of information and put two squiggly lines next to it! She obviously had no idea what she was writing and was just copying things off the board on autopilot. Had she really been listening to the lecture, she would have realized what he was doing and just written down the important information. The point: don't be a robot. Lots of important and interesting things go on in a lecture that never get written on the blackboard, and not everything that is written on the blackboard is important! More often than not, if the professor writes something on the board it is worth copying, but do pay attention.

A professor in a chemistry or physics course, for example, might occasionally do a demonstration in order to spice up the lecture and to illustrate a concept "in living color." The professor might make some potassium explode or dip a rubber ball in some liquid nitrogen and then shatter the ball on the floor. These demonstrations are designed to show you a concept in a shocking or amusing way, but don't forget the point of the demonstration! The professor obviously cannot write on the board while doing these demos, so don't forget to take notes. *Why* did the ball shatter after it was dipped in liquid nitrogen? This will be explained during the demo—write it down! The professor will want you to remember something important from this demo, not just to be amused.

Sometimes it might take a lengthy discussion, or several steps, or several equations, to get to the main point of a discussion. Write down the several steps or the several equations, keep them orderly, but *don't lose track of the main point.* You don't want to look back in your notes and see this series of steps which seem to have no direction and which lead nowhere. Not all lecturers are extremely well organized or extremely clear when presenting their material, but this does not mean that you can't take good notes in their classes. It does mean that you'll have to pay even greater attention to figure out the bottom line. If you have some sort of meandering discussion in your notes that never leads to a conclusion, then either you have a horrible lecturer or you missed something. Check the book, check with a friend, or go to the professor to find out what you missed. Again, *do this daily*—if you have a disorganized lecturer you will need to spend more time on your notes outside of class in order to make them coherent.

If you find that your lecturer is not presenting things well and not making it easy for you to take good notes, don't tune out; focus in even more, figure out what he or she is trying to say, and write it down. Or, write down what you *think* the professor is trying to say and then figure it out later. If it is confusing, don't just write nothing; write something and then get to the bottom of it with the help of friends, the teaching assistant (TA) assigned to the course, if there is one, or the book. In cases like this, it might be beneficial to read the appropriate section of the textbook *before* the lecture so that you have some idea of what the lecturer will be trying to say. Ordinarily, I recommend reading the book after the lecture, but if the lecture is hard to follow, reading the book ahead of time might be a good idea. Unfortunately, if you have a bad lecturer, it is *your* problem and you're going to have to deal with it and still learn something from this person. Your transcript will not have annotations next to bad grades received in courses that had bad lecturers! Good note-taking will help you get through courses like this. In cases of poor lecturing it is more important than ever to go over your notes daily and fill in details that were missing from the lecture. Don't be afraid to ask the professor to clarify, if not during the lecture, then during office hours. It is entirely possible that this person might not know that he/she is not getting through to people and needs to be more clear or provide more detail. Believe it or not, most professors like getting feedback from the students on how they come across in class. Be tactful in how you tell someone that he or she is not being clear. If you seem harsh or insulting, the professor might dismiss you as immature and unreasonable and it will not help your situation!

In some classroom situations it is not feasible to ask questions during the lecture, like if you are in a lecture hall with 500 people and you are sitting 50 yards away from the professor. But, if you are in a smaller class setting and the professor has expressed a willingness to take questions during the lecture, then by all means, do not be afraid to ask questions. Most students are afraid to speak up for fear of looking stupid. I have three things to say about this: first, if you already knew all of this material, you wouldn't be taking the course; it is new to you by definition, so it is not stupid to ask for clarification if something is unclear. Second, you are paying this person to teach you and you are entitled to ask questions—it is not an imposition. (It is rude to interrupt every five minutes, but an occasional question is certainly reasonable.) Third, if you have this question, it is very likely that at least one other person in the class is confused about the same thing and is also afraid to ask, so when you do ask, you will see relieved faces around you! Also, most professors enjoy an interactive class rather than a room full of zombies.

Some students prefer to use the professor's office hours to ask questions rather than asking them in class, and this is fine, provided you keep a couple of things in mind. First, stick to the posted times for office hours. Unless a professor says "sure, drop by any time," don't! If you can't make the office hours as they are scheduled, make an appointment. Next, have a list of questions ready; the more specific you are about what you don't understand, the better the professor will be able to help you. I recently had a student in my summer course come to office hours, sit down, and say "I don't get it." I said, "which part?" She said, "all of it." Now, this doesn't give me much to work with! No one can reconstruct the whole course during office hours, so please ask specific questions. Some professors provide an e-mail address to the class, and this is good for asking simple questions, but it is not good for asking for technical help because it's just too hard to explain how to do a science, math, or engineering problem via e-mail. Also, it's not good to use the e-mail for things like asking for exam grades over the weekend. Try to restrict the e-mail usage to things that you absolutely have to know before the next class, like what the homework problems were if you lost them, schedule changes during bad weather, or things of that nature.

Finally, getting back to taking notes, be singly focused on the lecture when you are in class. Don't be passing notes to your friend, working on something for another class, making social plans, or answering your cell phone, which shouldn't even be in the classroom (more later). Try to eliminate all distractions and just focus on the material at hand. Also, keep an organized notebook. You should have all of your class handouts, notes, homeworks, and exams together. A loose-leaf binder with pockets is best for this, or if you want to use a spiral notebook, have a folder for the other papers. Don't lose them or throw them away. This way you'll always know when your due dates and exam dates are and what the professor's rules and formats are, and you won't have to ask for information that has already been given out. Save everything that gets handed out in class! When I started teaching, the other professors told me that you have to say things three times before everyone will hear it. I thought this was ridiculous, but between people walking into class late (announcements are usually at the beginning of class), not coming to class at all, or not paying attention in class, it really is true. I once wrote the date and time for an exam on the board six times, starting a month before the final, and one student still missed the exam because she thought it was on Wednesday instead of Monday. I let her make it up because I'm a nice person (!), but I would have been well within my rights to say: too bad, I gave this information out six times. Don't let something like this happen to you. Make sure you know what is going on in your classes, and when final exam time comes around, make a calendar and check to be sure you have the dates right. If you miss a class, it is *your* responsibility to find out what you missed; it is not your professor's responsibility to take the initiative to inform you of what you missed. Attention to detail early on can avert disasters at the end of the semester!

A word about tape recorders: I don't recommend using them, but if you have a professor who is flying through material at an impossible speed and you just can't keep up with the note-taking, ask for permission to tape the lectures. Go over them after class at your own speed and make a good set of notes from the tape. The reason I don't recommend this method is because you can become too dependent on the tape and not develop good in-class note-taking skills as a result. Then, if you end up with a professor who says that you cannot tape his or her lectures, as some do, you will be stuck!

Chapter 4
Problem Solving

▶▶

Word Problems

Many science courses give word problems that ask you to solve for a certain quantity. The first step in dealing with word problems is to read them very carefully to make sure you understand exactly what they are asking for. This may sound obvious, but you'd be surprised at how many students get stuck right at the beginning because they are not focusing on what the problem is actually asking them to do. It is almost always useful to draw a picture or diagram. You don't need to be a good artist; just draw something that gives you an image of the situation depicted in the problem and what the problem is asking. Write down all of the known quantities in the problem and also write down all of the unknown quantities. Now, think of all the concepts that you studied that could possibly apply to this type of problem. Think of the equations you know. Oftentimes, in an introductory course, there will only be one or two equations that contain exactly the same variables and unknowns that you were given in the problem. Write down any appropriate equations and start trying to work with them to solve the problem. Many times, the problems students have solving technical word problems is that they are not creating a clear picture of what the problem is giving them and what the problem is asking for. If you follow the above method, you should be able to alleviate this situation. If you spend more than half an hour on a problem and get stuck, ask a friend (if this is allowed in your course) or go talk to the TA or professor. It could be that you are stuck on one little item that is blocking you from making progress on the rest of the problem and it would be a shame to leave the problem unsolved because of one sticking point. You don't need to ask how to do the whole problem; just explain the progress you've made, where you are, and ask for advice. You might be able to get a hint that will allow you to proceed without having the professor or TA give away the whole answer.

Another very useful thing to do when solving problems is to keep track of units: mass is in kilograms, time is in seconds, etc. Your professors will tell you to do this for exactness and correctness, but there are other reasons to do it as well; it can help you to get the right answer! For example, if you are solving a problem and you get to the bottom line, if you accidentally left something out of an equation, or accidentally included something that doesn't belong there, the final answer will turn out to be in the wrong units and you will notice this even if the number looks reasonable. If you get an answer that says Bobby was traveling at a speed of 10 pounds, you know you lost something along the way!

Finally, keep an eye on order of magnitude. Order of magnitude means a factor of 10, and by keeping an eye on order of magnitude I mean you should make sure the answer that you get is in the right ballpark for what you would expect. If the problem asks you to find a speed for an automobile and you get 15,000 mph, go back and check your math! This may sound silly, but I have seen students solve problems and get people weighing less than one pound and cars traveling near the speed of sound! Don't just "plug and chug." Look at your final answer and make sure it makes sense.

Problem-Solving Example

Here is a step-by-step example for the proper procedure to solve a technical problem.

Problem:

An object is placed 50 cm from a converging lens with a focal length of 25 cm. Find the location of the image formed by this lens.

Solution:

Step 1: What is the problem telling me and what is it asking for? It tells me that we have a converging lens with a focal length of 25 cm, and that an object is placed 50 cm in front of this lens. It then wants to know where the final image formed by this lens will be located. Questions to ask yourself: Do I know what a "converging lens" is? Do I know how to find the final image location given the focal length of the lens and the object location? If not, get answers to these questions before proceeding!

Step 2: Draw a sketch that turns the word problem into a picture describing the problem:

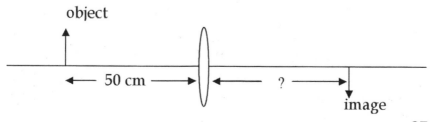

Step 3: Write down known and unknown quantities:
o = 50 cm (object distance from the lens)
f = 25 cm (focal length of lens)
i = ? (image distance from lens)

Step 4: Find an equation that uses all of these quantities and no others and that is appropriate to the problem: The lens equation: $\dfrac{1}{f} = \dfrac{1}{o} + \dfrac{1}{i}$ is appropriate.

Step 5: If the equation isn't arranged to solve for the variable you need, rearrange it before plugging numbers in: We need to solve for i, but the equation in its present form solves for f. Solve for i: $\dfrac{1}{i} = \dfrac{1}{f} - \dfrac{1}{o}$

$$i = 1 \Big/ \left[\dfrac{1}{f} - \dfrac{1}{o} \right]$$

Step 6: Plug in numbers and include units:

$$i = 1 \Big/ \left[\dfrac{1}{25cm} - \dfrac{1}{50cm} \right]$$

Step 7: Plug into calculator and solve for final answer:
Answer: i = 50 cm.

Step 8: Check units: image distance should be in distance units, and the final answer turned out to be in cm, so this makes sense.

Step 9: Check order of magnitude: Does it make sense that the image distance would turn out to be 50 cm, given that the object distance was 50 cm and the focal length of the lens was 25 cm? Yes, it looks reasonable. If the answer had turned out to be something like 1000 cm, you should go back and check the math. But, since the answer was the same *order of magnitude* as the original numbers in the problem, it looks reasonable even if you don't know anything about lenses.

This may look like a long, cumbersome way to solve a simple problem, but if you practice this method with the simple problems, it will become second-nature to you by the time you get to the more complicated problems where this method will be essential.

Working with Equations

When manipulating equations, start with the equation in algebraic form (meaning do not plug in any numbers yet) and solve for the unknown variable in the problem, as in the example above. When you get the equation into the proper algebraic form, *then* start plugging in the numbers. Otherwise, it is too easy to make a numerical mistake that you will not catch, and it makes it more difficult for the TA or professor to grade and less likely that you will receive partial credit for your work. It's far easier for a grader to figure out where you went wrong algebraically than by looking at a bunch of numbers. Also, if you leave the equation in algebraic form, you can make one last check to make sure that all the appropriate variables are included in the equation (you didn't lose anything) and that nothing is there that doesn't belong there. Check units! Again, all this is easier to do if you have not yet plugged in any numbers. This is universally true in science, engineering, and math courses.

Equation Example:

Problem:
Given the equation $f = \dfrac{1}{2L}\sqrt{\dfrac{T}{m}}$, find m (mass per unit length) if T = 100 Newtons (N), f = 300 Hertz (Hz), and L = 1.3 meters.

Solution:
For purposes of this example, don't worry about what this equation is for; we are just using it as an example of how to algebraically rearrange it and then plug in numbers. Start by solving the equation for m before plugging in any numbers:

Multiply both sides by 2L: $2Lf = \sqrt{\dfrac{T}{m}}$

Square both sides: $(2Lf)^2 = \dfrac{T}{m}$

Swap the m and (2Lf)² terms to get m by itself: $m = \dfrac{T}{(2Lf)^2}$

Now, plug in numbers and units:

$$m = \dfrac{100N}{\left[(2)(1.3meters)(300Hz)\right]^2}$$

Answer: m = 0.00016 kg/meter

A Newton is a unit of force equal to a kg*meter/second² and Hertz is a unit of frequency equal to 1/second, so you can see that the final answer units came out to be:

$$\dfrac{kg*meter \,/\, second^2}{meter^2 * second^2} = \dfrac{kg}{meter}$$

which is the proper unit for mass per unit length.

If you get stuck, start asking yourself questions so that you can pinpoint exactly what is confusing you. Start with what you definitely know, and keep getting more and more specific until you hit the part where you are stuck. In doing this, you might be able to solve your own problem, but if not, at least you will have isolated it to something specific so when you go to ask a question of your professor or TA, it will be the right question that will lead to the right kind of help for the problem. For example, in the above problem, maybe you knew that you had to get m by itself but you didn't know how to get rid of the square root sign. This is a specific question which you can ask someone and get a specific answer. If you just say "I don't know how to do this," it is hard to determine exactly what is troubling you and the person you asked may assume you know about the square root, and then you won't get the answer that you need.

You should do as many practice problems as you possibly have time for in a science, math, or engineering class. The more you practice, the easier this will become, because there is a limited number of types of problems you will encounter in any given course, and as you practice more and more, you will see the same trends popping up over and over in different problems. A technique or skill that you learn in solving one problem will definitely help you in solving future problems. Also, if you can, get a study group together and have each person work on a different problem and then explain it to everyone else. This will help all of you maximize your learning and use time efficiently.

Chapter 5
Studying for Exams

▶▶▶▶▶▶▶▶▶▶▶▶▶▶▶▶▶▶▶▶▶▶▶▶▶▶▶▶▶▶▶▶▶▶▶▶▶

Preparing for an exam really begins on the first day of the class. The key to good exam preparation is to keep current with the course material and not fall behind. On each day that the class meets, you should go home and go over your notes from that day. This can take as little as 10 to 15 minutes per day. Read through everything you wrote down and make sure that it makes sense. Oftentimes in class it is easy to write something down and think that it makes sense at the time, then later when you go back to look at it, you realize that you missed something. If you go over your notes each day, the lecture will still be fresh in your mind and you might be able to fill in the blanks just off the top of your head. If you can't, try looking in the textbook. If this doesn't work, call a friend in the class or go speak to the professor or TA the next time he or she has office hours. Definitely do not leave anything in your notes that you do not understand. This may sound time-consuming, but when it comes time for the exam this will cut down on your preparation time and alleviate stress because you won't feel "under the gun" to catch up on a large amount of material you do not understand. Doing a little bit each day is far better, both stress-wise and understanding-wise, than putting it all off until the week of the exam. When going through your notes, always ask the question of yourself: Why is this true? Do it with everything and leave no stone unturned in finding the answer. This will lead to a very thorough understanding of the material and will build confidence so that you won't go into an exam afraid that you will be asked something that you do not know.

In technical courses, it is very important to *understand* equations (not to memorize them!). Equations are not mathematical abstractions that are to be memorized and not understood. They are simply a language that is used to express a technical idea. Every equation can be expressed in words; you should look at each equation that was presented in the lecture and make sure that it makes sense to you. There are a couple of ways to do this. One way is to look at every variable in the equation and make sure that you understand why is there. If there is a factor of area or time in the equation, do you understand why that is there? Also, in equations, certain things will be proportional and certain other things will be inversely proportional. Make sure you understand why the things that are proportional are that way and why the things that are inversely proportional are that way. For example, if a certain quantity is decreasing with distance and that doesn't make sense to you, think about or look it up until you figure out why this is so. If you spend about half an hour and you still can't figure it out, go ask someone. Remember, you are not in this alone! Most professors would be thrilled to answer a conceptual question like "why is this quantity inversely proportional to distance?" because it shows that you are really thinking and that you care about understanding the material in the course. If a derivation (a step-by-step development) for an equation was presented in class or in the text, make sure you understand the derivation. This will tell you *why* the variables in the equation are in the positions that they are in. If parts of a derivation were given in class and steps were skipped, try to fill in those steps yourself—this is a great exercise.

Example of how to understand an equation: The Inverse-Square Law is a law of physics that applies to gravity, sound intensity, and electric force. For the case of gravity, the equation is:

$$F = G\frac{m_1 m_2}{d^2}$$

where F = force, G = gravitational constant, d = distance, and m_1 and m_2 are the masses of the two objects. Now, when presented with this equation in class, ask yourself this: Do I know what force means? Obviously we know what mass and distance are, but make sure you know what units you are using in this particular case (meters or centimeters, inches or feet). What is G? It is a constant that makes the units and magnitudes in the equation turn out correctly (otherwise known as a "fudge factor"—there are a lot of these in all branches of science. Just know that it is a constant and know its value). Next, say in words what this equation says in algebra: "The gravitational force is equal to the product of the masses of the two objects divided by the square of the distance between them, and this is all multiplied by the constant G." Next, ask yourself these questions: 1) Does it make sense that the gravitational force should be directly proportional to the masses of the two objects? Well, ok, if I have a larger mass, like the Earth, it will exert more gravity than a smaller mass, like myself. This makes sense. 2) Does it make sense that the gravitational force should *decrease* as the distance between two objects *increases*? Well, if an asteroid comes close to the Earth, it will be pulled in by the Earth's gravity, but if it stays farther away, it will not be pulled in. Gravitational force is weaker the farther away you get from the object exerting the force. Yes, this makes sense. Ok, so now you just verified this equation using every-day examples that you already understand. This is the method you should apply to all new equations that you encounter. Again, the more you do this, the faster and easier it will become. If you don't understand something, you will know specifically what you don't understand by asking yourself questions like the ones above and seeing if you can answer all of them.

Another great thing about understanding equations is that it cuts down on the need to memorize. If you understand something, you are much more likely to remember it than if it is just a meaningless collection of variables that you must commit to memory. If confronted with a specific problem during an exam and you can't remember the equation right away, having an *understanding* of the equations might trigger your memory once you determine exactly what the question is asking for. In the above example, you can see that it is easier to remember the inverse-square law once you understand the relationship between gravitational force, mass, and distance rather than trying to remember it by memorizing F, m, and d in the right order without regard for what they stand for.

The above discussion about equations also applies to concepts in non-technical courses, such as history. If you understand why an event happened or why someone did something the way he or she did, you will be less likely to need to memorize the facts. You will remember them because they make sense. Of course, certain things do need to be committed to memory, but you can cut down on memorization by increasing understanding.

When you are preparing for the exam, go through your notes and highlight the most important concepts and equations. Or, if you don't like highlighting, make separate study/summary sheets. Keep track of the big picture. There are certain trends in science and math that come up over and over again; you can begin to recognize them. Then, things are easier to remember (because you've seen something similar before) and things get tied together in a way that makes sense. Once you start seeing these connections, it helps to take the pressure off because everything doesn't seem so separate and disjointed. The inverse-square law is a great example of this; it says that certain quantities decrease as the square of your distance from the source increases. Once you understand the basic inverse square law, you will find that it works for sound, for light, and for gravity. Three ideas that you thought were unrelated now have this one law in common, and each time you see it you will recognize it and it won't be "another new thing" to learn. There are many other examples like this. Get the general ideas set in your mind first, and then work on the little details. To use an anal-ogy from history, if you are studying the Civil War, make sure you have an understanding of the main causes of the war before you worry about the details of specific battles.

Another important part of preparing for exams is doing practice problems. Most technical courses center on problem solving and, like learning a musical instrument, you will not become proficient at this if you do not practice. And, you will not become good at it by watching someone else do it. If there is a genius in your study group, do not let that person do all the work! If your course has assigned homeworks, take them seriously. They are they are to help you learn the material and prepare for the exams; in college, homework is not "busy work." In addition to the homework, most textbooks provide solutions to selected problems in the back to the book, or come with an accompanying student study guide. Do practice problems! Choose those where you can check your answers. When doing practice problems, try to form a study group with other students. You can learn a lot from one another by solving problems together, as long as everyone is contributing. Try having each person solve a problem and then explain it to the others; if you try to explain something to someone else, it is a great way to test your own understanding.

Use all resources available for the course. If the professor has created a web site, go look at it—there are probably links to related sites that can help you. If he/she has taken the time to create a web page, there definitely will be useful information on there. If you are lucky, the professor might have a set of course notes available, either online or in hard-copy format. Also look at suggested books that aren't the main textbook for the course.

This all sounds pretty time-consuming, right? That's why I said, in the chapter on choosing courses, to allow between 1—2 hours outside of class for every hour spent in class. But, there is a payoff. If you use this method of studying your notes each day, doing practice problems, and not leaving anything in your notes that you do not understand, when exam time comes around, it will not take that much time to prepare for the exam. You will not need to stay up all night cramming and memorizing and you will not be as stressed out. The rest of your life will not have to come to a screeching halt because you have an upcoming exam. This can be especially useful during midterms and finals when you have many exams in the same week. If you have kept up with the material, the night before the exam can be spent simply reviewing things that you already thoroughly understand, doing some practice problems, and committing some things to memory. People *do not* do better on exams by waiting until the last minute to start studying and by depriving themselves of sleep the night before the exam. This is not only a stressful practice that leads to poor performance, but it also does very little to help you remember the subject matter long-term. Presumably, you are taking this course because you'll need to know this information at some point in the future, either for another exam, another course, or for your career. Cramming things into short-term memory the night before an exam will not further any of these causes. Don't worry about what your friends are doing. Do the right thing - prepare early!

Finally, about your study environment: no matter what you did in high school, no matter what you are used to, no matter what your friends do, you MUST study in a quiet environment and *don't do anything else while you are studying*. This means no TV, no stereo, no stair-stepping while you are studying. These things are all distractions and will serve to lessen your ability to concentrate. (Some people think they help concentration but this just is not true.) The best way to do anything, even eating, is to do just one thing at a time and give that one thing your full attention. Practicing this will increase your powers of concentration, will help you remember what you read, and will help you to spend less time studying. You will then find it easier to take good notes in class and you will find yourself less distractible in general. If you "can't" study without music or the TV on, this might mean that you have a problem focusing and you should consider working on that. If focus is an issue for you, it will limit you eventually when you get to the really difficult courses. This doesn't mean that you can't do work on the bus on the way home, or sitting in the laundromat, but it means that these should not be your *primary* study locations. If you live in a dorm room or some situation where you can't get away from the noise and you don't want to go to the library, try a set of foam-rubber ear plugs. They will still allow you to hear important things like phones and alarms, but they will reduce the clatter from TVs, stereos, and people talking. This point about studying in a quiet place is the one I get the most flack about, but trust me, it works! Give it a try, not just for one day, and you'll grow to like it when you see the positive results it yields.

Chapter 6

Problem Solving on Exams

▶ ▶

When you are taking an exam that involves problem solving, especially one where partial credit will be given, it is extremely important for you to be clear in how you get from one step to the next. Think of how your page will look to someone who isn't inside your head! Don't make the grader try to figure out what you were thinking or struggle to follow your logic. Don't write in all different directions on the page and squeeze things in where there isn't enough room. The best approach is to start by writing down the knowns and unknowns, and then the relevant equation that you will use to solve the problem. Leave the equation in algebraic form until the last step, then plug in the numbers. This is the same procedure I outlined in the chapter on problem solving, and this will be easier for the grader to read, easier for you to make sure you don't make a careless mistake, and, if you make a mistake plugging in the numbers, it will be in the last step of the solution and you will be more likely to get more partial credit. Write legibly, and if your handwriting is bad, write large so it will be easier to read. Put a box around your final answer so that there is no doubt. Keep track of units, as always, and remember to make sure the bottom-line answer makes sense (order of magnitude). In the heat of the moment during an exam, it's easy to just get a number out of the calculator and write it down without making sure it isn't way out of line.

Remember that you can work the problems on the exam in any order you want; you do not have to do them in the order given (unless the instructor specifically tells you otherwise). You should look at all the problems and start by doing one which you feel is easiest. This will build your confidence and help get rid of some of those exam jitters. Do the easier problems first so that you can save time at the end for the more difficult ones. If you get stuck on a problem, put it aside, work on other problems, and then come back to the difficult one. You don't want to get hung up on a tough problem early in the exam while leaving the easier ones unsolved; it could very well be that the first problem on the exam is the most difficult one. If you do the difficult problems first, it will use up a lot of time and energy. This will lead you to rush at the end and possibly make a careless mistake on a problem that you otherwise could have mastered.

Don't let nervousness cause you to make careless errors. Take a deep breath, concentrate, check your work before you turn it in. If you are stuck on something and all the other problems are solved, try to just close your eyes for five minutes and relax. Sometimes things pop into your mind if you just give it a minute. Many times people come up with the answer right after they walk out the door. This is because the pressure is off and the knowledge breaks through the tension and comes to the surface. Try to get this to happen *before* you turn in the exam! I once had a student leave a note in my mailbox after an exam, saying that right after she turned in the exam, as she was walking to her car, she remembered how to do a problem that she had blanked out on in the room, and she wrote out the solution and asked me to include it with her exam and grade it! I didn't, of course. Had she sat back and relaxed a bit during the exam, the answer would have come to her then, instead of in the parking lot!

Never leave a problem blank on an exam. Even if you don't know how to solve it completely, write down anything that you do know that relates to the problem; you can pick up at least some partial credit this way. I don't mean that you should fill the page with unrelated information in an attempt to dazzle the professor with sheer volume, because that won't work, but there has to be something you can write that will show that you have some knowledge related to this problem. If you are totally clueless and can't write down anything relevant, then there is something wrong with the way you prepared for this exam!

I hate to even bring up multiple choice tests because I think they are totally inappropriate for college-level classes, but some professors who don't feel like grading real exams do use them. Never leave a multiple choice question blank. Always guess, even if you have no idea. If you have at least some idea, you can probably eliminate one or two choices and make an educated guess at the answer. The same goes for short-answer or fill-in-the-blank-questions—write *something*!

Write exams in ink unless you are told to do otherwise. There are two main advantages to this. First, if you want to go back and argue about how one of your problems was graded and you wrote in pencil and there are any erasures in that problem, you will be out of luck because you won't be able to prove that you didn't erase it after you got the exam back. Second, if you solved the problem correctly in ink, then crossed it out and solved it incorrectly, a kind grader might read the crossed-out correct version and give you credit for it! I wouldn't count on this, but it could happen. A third advantage is that no one else can alter what you wrote, should your exam become the victim of foul play. Unfortunately, exams do get lost or even stolen sometimes, and if yours ends up in someone else's hands before it gets to the professor, anything could happen.

A Word About Grades:

When you receive your exam grade, you might be happy with it, or you might not. If you are not happy with the grade, the thing to do is figure out where you went wrong and make corrections in your study methods. The thing *not* to do is to go to the professor and beg for points. Your exam was graded the same way as everyone else's and the professor cannot give points back to the one or two people who inevitably complain about the way the exam was graded. Partial credit is difficult and no matter how it gets done, someone always feels cheated. Get over it! It's not fair to ask for special treatment. Always remember that you are not the only person in the class and what gets done for you must get done for everyone or else it would not be fair. It doesn't matter how "important" the grade is to you; it is equally important to everyone else in the class. Trying to lay a guilt trip on the professor about how he/she is going to ruin your career if the grade is not changed is not going to win you any points, and it is an inappropriate thing to do. Also, don't go to the professor with scenarios like "if I get an A on the final can I still make a B for the course," etc. The professor cannot make predictions about grades, so don't ask!

A Word About Academic Honesty:

It goes without saying that you should never cheat on an exam, lab report, or anything else, but if you are the person being copied *from* it can be a difficult situation. My advice is, no matter how close you think a friend is or no matter what the excuse, do not *ever* let anyone copy your work. People might try to pressure you, and you might feel obligated or afraid that you will lose a friend if you don't let them cheat. Most people would get over it and respect your decision; certainly anyone who genuinely cared about you would not put you in that position. If someone refuses to be your friend because you did not let him/her cheat from you on an exam, then you're not losing much of a friend and you're probably better off getting a person like that out of your life, even if it is painful at first. Some people go through life sponging off of others. Don't be a victim. Bad feelings eventually fade, but if you get caught cheating, you could fail the course and/or have a notation on your transcript about academic dishonesty which will follow you for the rest of your career. Most professors don't care which person is the copier and which person is allowing the copying; both are guilty of cheating and the professor will have little sympathy for arguments about peer pressure. Once you get caught doing something like this (and believe me, it is *so* easy to tell when work has been copied) your reputation with that professor will be destroyed and you won't be able to talk your way out of the situation. Put your foot down, say no, cover your paper, and you'll feel better about it later.

Also, don't make up stories or lie to your professor in order to get a make-up exam or an extension on a deadline. Professors are used to dealing with all kinds of special situations and, if you are an honest, hard-working student, a reasonable person should be willing to cut you some slack if you are having a special problem. Even if it is something less extreme than a death in the family or an illness, tell the truth. It is pretty easy to tell when someone is lying, so you most likely will be found out if you try this, and then you will lose the respect of your professor. Also, it is very hard to cover all the bases when you are making up a story, so it's best not to try! The following joke illustrates my point:

Four physics students had an exam on Monday morning, but they stayed up late Sunday night drinking at the fraternity house, and on Monday morning they didn't feel like taking the exam. "I know," one said, "we'll tell the professor that we went away for a funeral over the weekend and got a flat tire on the way home, and that's why we missed the exam." So, they went to the professor with this story and asked for a make-up exam. "No problem," said the professor. He put each student in a separate room and gave them each an exam. The first page, worth 5 points, was a very easy one-dimensional motion problem which they all knew how to do. "Great," they thought, "this is going to be easy!" They each then flipped to page 2, which read: "95 points: which tire?"

Finally, the issue of academic integrity is becoming more prominent on college campuses because of the common usage of the internet for research. Always remember that if you get information from *any* source, including the internet, and use it in your work that you turn in for a grade, you *must* give credit to the original author. Failure to do so constitues plagirarism, which is a serious offense.

It is not acceptable to cut and paste things from the internet into a paper that you are writing and imply that it is your own original work by not citing the original author(s). Professors are keenly aware of this problem, and software programs exist to help professors catch students plagiarizing work from the internet, so don't try to get away with copying anything from anywhere without giving credit. When in doubt, cite a reference.

Chapter 7
Laboratory Exercises

▶ ▶

One of the keys to success in a course with a lab component is to prepare ahead of time by reading the lab exercise before you arrive so that you know what questions to ask before the procedure begins. Many lab exercises are very time-consuming and will require the bulk of the lab session to complete; if you don't know what you are doing going in, you might not have time to finish and you will feel rushed. Also, you need to know what equipment to bring with you: a calculator, a protractor, maybe a timer of some sort.

When you get into the lab room the equipment will be set up for you in proper working order. *Do not touch anything until the instructor tells you how to use the equipment.* It never ceases to amaze me how many people will walk into a lab room and start pressing buttons on a $15,000 piece of equipment that they have no idea how to use! The instructor should run through the lab procedure and introduce you to any new equipment that will be used, and then you can get started. Colleges have very limited budgets to replace damaged lab equipment, so please be kind to the equipment. Do not try to use it in any way other than its intended mode of operation.

Read through the entire lab procedure before you start to do anything. Sometimes the lab procedures are unclear or might be missing a step. You don't want to find this out when you are in the middle of something, like mixing chemicals or building a circuit. If anything in the step-by-step is unclear, ask the instructor before you begin. Then you should be able to carry out the procedure smoothly and get good data without any confusion or interruptions. Think before you act!

Safety is a major concern in any lab course. Be mindful of everything you do in the lab. You could hurt yourself or someone else if you are not paying attention or if you are trying to do something with the equipment that is outside of its normal use. The safety rules and procedures should be told to you by your lab instructor, but I will remind you of some basics: never point a laser at anyone and never look directly into a laser; never touch any chemicals without the proper gloves and eye protection; never touch an electrical circuit without checking first to see if the power supply is cut off. Make sure equipment or chemicals are standing firmly on the lab bench, and not on the edge, so that they can't tip over or be easily knocked over. Don't leave lab stools in the middle of the aisle where people can trip over them. Wipe up spills immediately and if you get exposed to *any* chemicals, tell the instructor immediately and take the proper first-aid steps. Do not just ignore it and assume it will be ok. Some chemicals go right through the skin and attack the bone and you don't even realize it until hours later, and then it is too late. Always err on the side of caution in the lab, whether you're working with chemicals, lasers, biological specimens, or electricity.

Take your time and don't rush when working in the lab; rushing leads to accidents. Also, never start any horseplay in the lab. A friendly shove out on the quad in response to some teasing might be fine, but in the lab it can lead to disaster. There's a time and a place for everything, and when you are in a science lab, it's time to be serious and careful.

Take data in a neat and organized way so that when you go to write up the lab report, possibly a few days later, you will know what you are looking at! If you just scribble numbers on a piece of paper and don't label anything or keep it in order, you will have a very hard time writing your lab report, and your lab partners will not be able to understand what the data is. Take the few extra seconds to label things and write some extra detail— you'll be glad you did.

Don't let your lab partner dominate the experiment; some people are more naturally passive than others and can end up in a lab group where a dominant person takes over and the passive person just sits there. Don't let this happen to you. Labs are a great opportunity to get hands-on science experience and you won't get that many opportunities in your life. You can't learn to ride a bike by watching someone else do it, and you won't learn as much from a lab by being a spectator. Don't let anyone cheat you out of the experience that you are entitled to; lab procedures should be equally shared among all partners. Speak to the instructor if you are having a problem. Don't just let it go.

Before you leave the lab, make sure you've followed all the procedures, gotten all the required data, and are prepared to answer all the questions in the lab manual. Once you are sure you have everything you need, turn off all your equipment and leave the lab bench in a safe and orderly condition. Throw away any trash you may have accumulated during the session. If any equipment broke or was not functioning properly while you were using it, alert the instructor—do not just leave it for the next lab group to discover the hard way!

Here are some tips for taking good data:

- Don't use the very end of a ruler to start a measurement; the end is rough and will lead to inaccuracies. Start the measurement at, say, the one cm mark;

- When changing anything in the experiment, wait a few seconds for the apparatus to settle down before you take any measurements;

- Make changes - like turning up the current, adding weight, or pouring chemicals - slowly, not in a jerky or fast manner;

- Don't lean on, sit on, or bump the lab table during the experiment;

- Make sure the equipment is zeroed properly before you use it. This means that a balance should read zero grams when there is no object sitting on it, and a light power meter should read zero watts when no light is hitting it;

- Make sure that any moving parts in the experiment are free to move the way they are supposed to; if something seems to be hung up or not moving freely, alert the instructor;

- If performing a measurement that contains a lot of uncertainty, perform it two or three times and take the average value;

- If troubleshooting, change only one thing at a time and then re-check the results;

- Write down everything that you do that deviates from the written lab procedure so that you can include it in your conclusion when discussing discrepancies and problems;

- Look over your data when you are finished; if there are any anomalous points, you might want to repeat your measurement for that point;

- If you are doing any kind of experiment that involves measurement of light, make sure there is no stray light hitting your detector, such as overhead room lights, or light from the windows. You should use a black cloth or some kind of enclosure to shield your experiment from stray light;

- If you are building an electric circuit, make sure all of your connections are solid, don't use any more wires than are necessary, and spread things out on the breadboard so it is easy to analyze the circuit. If the circuit does not work, check all connections first and then swap out components one at a time, checking the circuit each time;

- When using any piece of equipment that has different scales, such as a light power meter, an ammeter, or a voltmeter, make sure that you are on the appropriate scale for your measurement. The needle should not be pinned at the high end or hovering at the low end; change scales if this is happening. If it is a digital meter, avoid small decimal numbers with many zeros or large numbers that fill the entire display. You should try to stay in the middle of the range for whichever scale you have chosen.

Above all, listen to your lab instructor and follow his/her advice. A helpful hint from an experienced person can save you a lot of agony in the lab! Even if you think you know a better way to do something, or if a procedure looks "stupid" to you, take the advice of someone more experienced than yourself and do it the way they tell you to do it. You can definitely question why it is being done in a specific manner if it seems strange to you, but don't deviate from instructions or advice given by the lab instructor.

Chapter 8
Writing Lab Reports

▶ ▶

In most technical courses, the laboratory portion of your grade will be based upon your written lab report. Just as it is important to do a good job of taking data in the lab, it is equally important to analyze that data and write up your results in a clear and intelligent manner. I have had students who have gone through great pains to take good data in the lab only to spend almost no time on the lab write-up, resulting in a poor grade. Once you complete the lab, you must be able to effectively communicate the results.

Your instructor should give you a format for your lab reports. Make sure you follow this format every time you write a report. Every good lab report, however, requires analysis of the data and a conclusion explaining the main results of the lab, any discrepancies in the data compared to the theory, and an explanation for such discrepancies. Make sure that you put some thought into your conclusion. Show your instructor that you know how to look at experimental results and draw intelligent conclusions from them. A lab report is not busy-work; do not spend time re-copying "objectives" and procedures from the lab manual unless your instructor specifically tells you to do so, which, in my experience, most college-level instructors will not do. We all know that you have the ability to read and copy; the purpose of a lab report is to see if you can think! For example, you do an experiment in which you're supposed to be able to produce a note of a certain frequency on a string. You do your calculation using the theory, you do the experiment and take your data, and the theory and experimental results do not agree. More often than not, this is what will happen when you do a lab. It's not necessarily because you did anything wrong, it's just the nature of experimental work. The key to getting a good grade in a lab report is coming up with an intelligent explanation for why the data did not agree with the theory—don't just state that it didn't agree and leave it at that. Think about it, analyze it, take your best guess, but write something original about what you think was going on in the experiment. In most lab courses, you don't need perfect data in order to get a good grade. It's what you do with the data that matters more!

The quality of your writing is also an important component of a lab report. Since scientific concepts are often difficult to communicate, it is all the more important that you have the ability to express your ideas clearly. Your writing should have a logical flow and should lead to a definite conclusion. It should also be typed or written in very neat handwriting so that your instructor does not have to struggle to read it. Your data should be clearly labeled so that the instructor knows what he/she is looking at. Don't just assume that the instructor will "figure it out" because he/she is familiar with the experiment. If the data you took during the lab session got messy, then rewrite it for the final lab report. If this is not allowed, then make sure you take neat data the first time around. If you made any charts or graphs, label all axes with the quantity and the units. If you made multiple charts or graphs with the same quantities on the x and y axes, explain what is different about the graphs—what did you change from one to the next in order to get the new data? Ideally, someone who was not in this lab should be able to read your report and have a clear understanding of what the lab was about and what your data revealed. Keep this in mind while you are preparing the report; it will help to make sure you include enough detail and present things clearly. I once had a student come up to me, weeks after a lab report was due, with two coffee-stained, sloppy pieces of paper with illegible numbers scribbled all over them. This was apparently data (which was not labeled at all) that he had taken in a lab session weeks earlier. He said to me "I can't make heads or tails out of this," and then looked at me like I was supposed to figure out what these numbers were. Of course, I could not. I told him, "YOU took the data; if you don't know what it is, how am I supposed to know?"

This brings up an important point: work on your lab report as soon after the lab session as possible so that everything is still fresh in your mind. Assuming the lab report is due at the next lab session, come to class with all the pieces written, assembled, and stapled. Don't be copying data from a lab partner, scribbling a quick conclusion, and trying to find a stapler while class is supposed to be in session; this should all be taken care of before you come to class. Above all, do not copy conclusions from your lab partners or anyone else. Data, of course, must be shared among lab partners, but the conclusion must be in your own words. You will not learn anything from copying a conclusion from someone else, and believe me, you *will* get caught! A conclusion in a lab report helps you to build several skills; it makes you analyze, organize, summarize, create a logical flow of ideas, and write coherently. Don't give up the chance to work on all these skills by giving it short-schrift or trying to copy it from somewhere. The more of these you write, the better you will get at it, the less time it will take, and the better your writing in your other classes will become.

Chapter 9
Writing Technical Papers

▶ ▶

The same rules which apply to writing a good paper in any subject also apply to writing technical papers. The two most important factors are having a logical flow of ideas and expressing those ideas in a clear and coherent manner. As with all papers, you should start with an outline. A technical paper should have an abstract, an introduction, a background theory section, a main body containing the results, and a conclusion. This is the general format for peer-reviewed technical papers which get published in refereed scientific journals. If you plan a career in science, it is good to get used to this format. Your instructor might provide a different format, which of course you should follow for that particular course.

The abstract should be a short summary of the main results of the paper, it should tell a person who is not familiar with your paper what your main results were in very few words but in specific detail. The abstract should provide enough information to the readers to help them decide if they want to read your paper. It should be very clear and to the point so that someone who is searching through a large number of abstracts can determine the main point of your paper quickly.

The introduction should explain the basics of your project and the motivation for doing the project. It should get your reader familiar with the current state of knowledge in the subject area and why you chose to pursue the topic under discussion. You can cite previous research published by other authors and point out the previous lack of the information that you are about to present in the current literature. The introduction sets the stage and should get the reader excited about the results you are about to present. It motivates the discussion that follows.

The background theory section is designed for readers who are either new to your research area or are experts in a somewhat related area. Start this section off at some reasonable level of theory that you think most of your readers can pick up on and provide enough detail from there so that when you present your results, the reader will have the necessary theoretical background to understand the results.

The main results section of your paper is where you present new theories, experimental data, and conclusions that you drew from your work. If your work is theoretical, provide a detailed, logically flowing explanation of your theory. Pause at each step and make sure you haven't made too great a leap for someone who has not been working on this every day for several months. Tell a continuous story from start to finish. If your research is experimental, describe the experimental apparatus in detail, using pictures and diagrams if possible. Describe your method of data collection and then describe the results clearly. Any charts, tables, or graphs should be clearly labeled; do not force your reader to "figure out" what they are looking at. On graphs, always label axes and include units. Explain the connections between your data and your conclusions. Do not assume it is obvious. Also explain things that you ruled out during the experiment: "this effect could not be caused by . . . because . . . "By the time your reader finishes your results section, he/she should have no question as to what you did, how you did it, why you drew your conclusions, and what those conclusions were. A competent experimentalist should be able to reproduce your experiment based on your paper.

The conclusion section should tie it all together: the motivation for pursuing the project, the previous lack of this information in the published literature, the new information provided by your research, and its overall significance to the scientific community. The conclusion section should also contain acknowledgments of coworkers, sponsors, and facilities where the work was performed.

Pay attention to detail in your writing. Make sure you don't leave out any steps in any of your technical explanations. Diversify your language so that you are not using the same words over and over. Avoid vague words and phrases like "not that much" or "a little bit" unless you can back them up with some description. Also avoid ambiguous words that can have more than one meaning. Don't jump around from point-to-point; when you start explaining something, stick with it until the explanation is complete, and then change the subject. Don't use more words that are necessary; be succinct. If your writing meanders from point-to-point or takes forever to get to the point, you will lose your reader's interest and possibly your reader's understanding. If you use any terms that are unique to your field, define them first. If you assume too high a level of specialty on the part of your reader, you will lose readers. Always present the reasons behind the results, whether they are experimental or theoretical. Explaining why something happened is as important as reporting that it happened at all. Spell and grammar-check your paper when it is finished. Make sure any equations have all variables defined.

It is very important that you use the proper format for your citations (references). Currently, the three most common formats are MLA, Turabian, and APA. Style manuals are available for each of these. Either your school, your professor, or the journal to which you are submitting a paper will specify which format is preferred or required. Familiarize yourself with the format and start using it immediately. If a format is not specified, choose one that you like and use it consistenly. Finally, have someone who is familiar with your subject area and who has good writing skills proofread your paper, and be willing to make changes based on constructive criticism. You might even try reading the paper aloud, or better yet, having someone else read it aloud to you. This will enable you to hear the paper in a different way than you would "hear" it if you were reading it to yourself.

Chapter 10
Dealing with Math

▶ ▶

Dealing with math is mostly an issue of mind over matter. Students who have trouble with math usually have set up a mental block because they have psyched themselves out and convinced themselves that they "can't do math." Maybe it started with poor instruction in high school or before; maybe it is a matter of self-esteem. In many cases, just getting over the fear of approaching math can be more than half the battle. Getting over the rest of it takes concentration, practice, and some decent guidance from a tutor or teacher. It's like walking into a gym for the first time and saying "I can't lift weights." Sure, if you've never tried to lift weights, if you don't go to the gym regularly, if you've never been taught how to lift weights, or if you tried to do it yourself the wrong way and hurt yourself, then yes, you can't lift weights. But, if someone teaches you the major do's and don'ts and you diligently stick to a regular schedule of workouts, then you will be able to lift weights. It's the same with math. First, convince yourself that math is something that you *can* do if you put in the proper effort. Math is simply a symbolic way of representing ideas; it is the language of science. There's no reason to fear learning a new language! Forget any bad experiences you may have had in the past; start with a clean slate.

If math has historically been a stumbling block for you but you need to pursue technical courses to get your degree, it is best, right at the beginning of the semester, to speak to the professor for whatever math course you are taking and let him/her know that you tend to have difficulty with this subject. Ask what additional resources, beyond the normal course materials, are available and recommended. You should probably also get a tutor or go to the math help center on your campus, if there is one, right away. Don't delay: if this is a problem for you, you need to tackle it straight on and without any hesitancy. Also, when you go to a tutor or the professor to ask for help, try to be as specific as possible about what is troubling you. This will require some detective work on your part; is it that you don't understand what the problems are asking, that you understand what they are asking but don't know which skill to apply, or, you know which skill to apply but don't know how to apply it? The more specific you can be when asking for help, the greater the chance that you will get the help you need. It's like going to the doctor and telling him/her that you are in pain—it helps a lot if you can describe where it hurts!

The methods for taking notes and studying for exams that are detailed in this book are completely applicable to math courses. However, here are some ideas that apply especially to math courses. When you are learning math, you are building a set of skills. Each time a math skill is taught, you should do many, many practice problems to make sure you understand this skill completely. This is like doing reps in the weight room. Practicing math skills builds the analytical part of your mind; the more you practice, the better you will get. As soon as you don't understand something, go get help. Don't let it slide, because most math skills build on one another, and if you let something slide in the beginning, it will come back to haunt you later. When you look at a math problem, ask yourself: "What is this problem asking me to do? Which skill must I apply to this problem?" People often see a problem and freeze because they don't know how to proceed. Don't let this happen; determine exactly which area of the recent class material is being tested by this question, and then apply the appropriate skill. This goes back to what I discussed in the problem-solving section: make sure you know exactly what the question is asking you to do.

Being able to successfully apply the skill and obtain the right answer is just a matter of practice. There's no magic to it. Just do practice problems over and over, and your skills will improve. There are a limited set of math skills that you will need to get through any particular math course, and more than likely, you'll see the same set of skills come up over and over again. Learn to recognize similarities in problems so that you can apply skills you have already mastered. Don't try to reinvent the wheel when you don't have to. For example, if you are taking an introductory calculus course, you'll learn to take derivatives. Once you understand the skill of taking a derivative, you'll have that skill at your disposal no matter what kind of derivative problem is thrown at you. The purpose of doing practice problems is to encounter different variations on how the same skill may be applied in a variety of situations. This way, on an exam, you are unlikely to run into a situation that you cannot handle. The same holds true for the much simpler situation of solving an equation for a particular variable (see example in Chapter 4). Once you master the skill of being able to solve any equation for any variable, no matter what that variable's position in the original equation, you'll be able to apply that skill no matter what the professor puts on the exam. Remember to keep your eye on the big picture - the set of skills - and not get bogged down in specific examples. If you try to just memorize specific examples, you won't have the skill set and you won't do well on the exam.

Example:
Solve the following equation for x:
$3x^2 + 7x—2 = 0$.

Solution:
Step 1: Determine which skill is needed to solve this problem. Answer: This problem asks you to solve a quadratic equation for the variable x, so the quadratic formula must be used.

Step 2: Write down the necessary formula:

$x = -b \pm \dfrac{\sqrt{b^2 - 4ac}}{2a}$ where in this case a = 3, b = 7, and c = 2.

Step 3: Plug the numbers into the formula to get the final answer:

$x = -2 \pm \dfrac{\sqrt{7^2 - (4*3*2)}}{2*3}$ = -2.83 or -1.16.

Discussion:
Notice the method used to solve this problem. In step 1, we determined what the question was asking us to do:

which skill is required? In step 2, we determined which formula was necessary, and in step 3, we applied the formula to find the answer. Usually, students will have trouble with one of these steps more so than another. Maybe you have a problem determining what the question is asking. If this is the case, slow down, re-read the question, and take it one step at a time. Once you have put into your own words what the question is asking, you next need to find the appropriate formula. Usually problems in a textbook use formulas from the same chapter where the problem is found, and sometimes the problems are even divided up into sections of the corresponding chapter. This greatly limits the number of potential formulas to use, so you should be able to find the correct one. Of course, on an exam, there is a much broader choice of formulas, but by the time you take the exam, if you have done many practice problems, finding the right formula should be easy. Finally, step 3 requires the proper use of the formula. You have to know what the variables stand for and what numbers to plug in. Again, practice should help take care of this if this is a problem for you. If you get hung up on any one of these steps consistently, you can go to the professor, TA, or tutor, tell them exactly what is troubling you, and then you can get specific help.

So you see, no matter what level of math you're at, the key is to overcome your fear, master the skills one by one as they are presented, and practice them. Keep up with the work, be diligent, and don't allow yourself to fall behind. Don't try to learn by example without mastering the underlying concepts; you'll get lost in the details of specific examples and miss the point. Spend a lot of time on this if you need to. As you improve, it will become less time-consuming. And, as always, get together with friends and work on problems together!

Lastly, try not to use your calculator or computer for absolutely everything. I see students who have to divide something by 10 and they go right to the calculator. By the time you are past elementary school, this is something that you should be able to do in your head without even thinking about it, so when simple operations like this come up, do it in your head, not on the calculator. This will help keep your mind sharp.

Chapter 11

Dealing with Professors: Some Things That You Shouldn't Say or Do

▶▶▶▶▶▶▶▶▶▶▶▶▶▶▶▶▶▶▶▶▶▶▶▶▶▶▶▶▶▶▶▶▶▶▶▶

If I were to sit here and hypothetically come up with a list of statements that would annoy me, if said by a student, it would probably look a little different from the list here, but what is presented here are all statements that have been said to me more than once by students I have had. This is the sort of stuff that early retirement is made of! Now, I'm not saying that every single professor out there feels the same way about these things that I do, but it is a pretty safe bet that most of these things are not good to do. Here's a list of some of the most annoying things students say/do that I highly recommend you avoid:

1. "If I don't get at least a B in this course I will fail out of school, so keep that in mind when you're grading my exam." Grades are based on performance, not sympathy. Do not try to lay on a guilt trip of any kind.

Of course it is important to you if you do or don't fail out of school, get into medical school, graduate school, graduate with honors, or whatever you goal is, but realize that a professor cannot take this into consideration when determining your grade. Your grade is based on your performance in the class as outlined in the syllabus, and that's the *only* determining factor.

2. "Can I do an extra credit project to raise my grade?" Sounds like: "I couldn't be bothered to learn this material for the exam, so now I want to make more work for you and get an easy way to raise my grade." If you end up doing poorly in a class, you have to accept it and move on. Figure out why you did poorly and take steps to correct it. You can't look for a quick-fix like trying to write a paper to make up for a whole semester's worth of poor performance. It's not a reasonable request because if the professor lets you do it, then he/she would also have to extend the option to everyone who didn't get an A, because everyone wants a higher grade. If a professor wants to give extra credit opportunities, he/she will probably announce this, and if not, it is better not to put the professor in the awkward position of having to say no to you when you're asking something that should not be asked, especially at the end of the semester when there is already so much grading to be done without any extras.

3. "A C- won't transfer to my school—can you make it a C?" This makes me think: Why bother having exams then? Just tell me what grade you want and I'll give it to you. This is a ridiculous request which I get every time I teach summer school. Again, your grade is determined from your performance on the exams and other course requirements and does not depend on what you are going to do with that grade afterwards. If your school won't accept a C- then make darn sure you don't *earn* a C-! Remember, the professor didn't *give* you that grade—you earned it.

4. "I know you said you wouldn't change the partial credit on the exam, but I think I deserve more points for this answer." Sounds like: "I'm special—the rules are for everyone else." Partial credit is a very difficult thing to determine fairly, and once it has been decided how it will be doled out, it gets doled out the same for every student who made the same mistake. Don't ask for special treatment. I personally put enormous effort into making sure the way I assign partial credit is fair and self-consistent. That means, upon looking at all of the exams, there is a range of errors and a range of points deducted for specific errors. The same standard is applied to everyone, and that's what makes it fair. When you look at your exam and maybe the exams of 2 or 3 friends, you are not getting the full picture, so it is easy for you to sit there and decide that the grade is unfair. What you have to remember though is that the points that were deducted for your error were also deducted from *everyone else* who made the same error, and that's why it is fair. You might quibble with the amount of the deduction, but that is a decision made by the professor that you'll have to live with. No matter what amount is chosen, someone will always complain because the bottom line is, people don't like losing points on an exam, no matter what the amount is.

If the course is curved or scaled in any way, which most college technical classes are, then the actual amount of the deduction doesn't mean that much because it will be "corrected" to a certain extent at the end of the course when the scaling or curving is applied. In other words, the straight number grade that you receive doesn't mean the same thing in a scaled course as it does on a straight

65

scale (where 65 is failing, etc.). For example, let's say I give an exam and on one question a bunch of people make the same error and I take off 10 points for that error. Let's also say that at the end of the course I am going to set the class average equal to a B. When the students see the grade for that one problem, they come complaining to me, saying that instead of 10 points, I should have only taken off 5 points. Well, it really doesn't matter because if I take off 10 points, the class average will be a little bit lower than it would have been if I had only taken off 5 points, but it will still be equal to a B in the end, so it all comes out in the wash. The bottom line is, it doesn't matter what the numerical grade is, only the final assigned letter grade matters, so don't lose sleep over 5 points on one exam if practically everyone else also lost the same 5 points!

5. "I know you said not to come by between 5 and 6 o'clock, but I have just one quick question." Stick to posted office hours. Professors are human beings who need time away from the course, even if they are still in the office. If they ask you not to come by at certain times, then respect that. You might think it's just "one quick question," but remember that there might also be 20 other people with "one quick question," and that adds up and becomes unmanageable for the professor if everyone acts like he/she is the only one in the course!

6. "Can you make the exam multiple choice?" NOT appropriate at college level! This is like saying "I don't want to have to think on this exam—make it easy." It's always bad to communicate a desire to be lazy or disinterested in learning, and asking for a multiple-choice exam is a sure-fire way to turn off your teacher!

7. "What do we have to know this for anyway?" You never know when something you learned will come in handy; keep an open mind. You might make a career change that will suddenly require you to know all sorts of things you never expected to need. You might decide to teach! Besides, it's good to learn things just for the sake of learning them—it helps your mind to grow, and this is beneficial no matter what career you end up in. And again, a negative statement like this one puts a dagger in the heart of a teacher who has a genuine interest in the subject material!

8. "If we just study the homework problems will that be ok for the exam?" Sounds like: "I don't really want to learn all this stuff; narrow it down for me." It's better to just study what was taught than to try to corner the professor into narrowing down what will be on the exam. The professor expects you to learn all the material that was taught, not just selected portions of it. Yes, it is a lot to learn, but we all had to do it!

9. "Why does the final have to cover the WHOLE course?" Because that's what finals do; you have to show that you learned ALL the material. Again, a statement like this shows laziness and a lack of interest in learning and will totally turn off the teacher. If the professor is going to give a cumulative final, then that's what he/she has decided is best for that course, and making comments like this won't change that fact.

10. "If I have a C- average going into the final and I ace it, can I still make a B in this course?" Don't ask your professor to guess at what your grade will be. If you know what the relative weighting for the different exams will be, then punch some numbers into the calculator and figure it out for yourself. If the course is curved or scaled, then there's no possible way for the professor to predict what the class average will be and what grade it will take to get an A in the course. For example, if I decide to set the final class average equal to a B, it could turn out that the class average is a 65, or it could turn out that it is an 80. In this case, it is impossible to predict ahead of time what numerical grade will end up corresponding to an A.

11. This one's not a quote, but I must say something about students who sit in class and talk and fool around the whole time, as if I can't hear this and don't notice this. Believe me, *your professor knows what you are doing in class*. If you are making fun of him/her, if you are bored, if you are being disrespectful . . . it is *so* easy to perceive this, even when one's back is turned, even in a large class. This will be remembered if you need any special favors, like if you are sick during the midterm, or whatever else may come up. Be respectful in class.

12. A word about cell phones . . . DON'T BRING THEM TO CLASS!!! Being respectful includes not bringing cell phones and pagers to class; this is disruptive and unnecessary! No one is so important that he/she can't be out of touch with the outside world for an hour. I don't care what the excuse is; if you can't get someone else to take care of it for you while you are in class and it is a dire emergency, then skip class that day and take care of it, whatever it is. Otherwise, it can wait! This goes back to what I said about distractions in the chapter about studying for exams. When you are in class, just be in class—don't have your mind elsewhere. Generations of students before you, including mine, got by just fine without having phones ringing in class. We got our messages a little later and the world did not come to a catastrophic end, so please learn to be less dependent on these darn phones!

Chapter 12:

Special Situations: Summer Courses, Extra Help, Online Courses, Hardships

▶ ▶

Summer Courses

Summer courses can be a double-edged sword. Students often use them to try to get ahead in their program, or to make up for lost time because of a change in major, or if they had to drop a course during the year for some reason. Taking technical courses during the summer session is extremely difficult because an entire semester's worth of material is packed into six weeks. This means that the pace of the course is more than twice as fast as it is during the normal school year. If you are well-organized, can stay on top of the work, are not weak in the subject area, and can devote a lot of time to the course, then you can do well in a summer course. However, if you are looking to take a course in a subject that does not interest you and in which you tend not to do well, trying to take it over the summer to "get it over with" is not a good idea. One summer course which includes a lecture and a lab is like a full-time job in itself. It is best to try not to take more than one at a time or to try to also have a full-time job while you are taking the course. Be prepared for a lightning-fast pace and a heavy time commitment if you plan to take summer courses.

If you are not taking the summer course at your normal school, make sure you understand exactly what the requirements are for transferring credit to your school and satisfying the requirements for your major. For example, if you are required to take physics, must you take calculus-based physics, or can you take algebra-based physics? Is there a laboratory requirement? Make sure you find out these things before you register for the course. Also, make sure that your summer course does not overlap with either the spring or fall semesters at your regular school. If you have to join the course a week late or leave a week early, you are not just missing a week, you are missing more like two and a half weeks because of the compressed schedule. In a technical course, this can be very difficult to overcome, so you should consider it very seriously if the schedules do overlap.

Extra Help

If you have applied all of the study methods described in this book and you are still having trouble with the course, you might need to seek extra help. You should, of course, go to your professor's and TA's office hours, but if you need more help than can be provided in this setting, you might need to seek outside resources. The first thing you should do in seeking extra help is to recognize the situation early on and not wait too long before you look for help. A tutor cannot turn things around for you overnight, and if you wait until two weeks before the final to find one, it's too late.

There are several ways that you can seek out extra help in a technical course. First, be sure to use all the resources suggested by the professor: books, web sites, etc. Another way is to use the internet on your own; there are several web sites which provide tutorials in technical subject areas. Be sure to make use of the instructional support services available at your school. Sometimes this is done centrally to accommodate a variety of subject areas, and sometimes it is handled by the individual departments. Look in your college catalog or speak to the department for the course in which you need help to find out what kind of instructional support is available. Finally, you can hire a private tutor. It is best to find someone who comes highly recommended with a proven track record of success. Ask around; don't just answer the first flier you see on a bulletin board.

Online Courses

Distance learning is a growing trend at many colleges and universities these days, and there are a variety of formats for online courses. Some use video-taped presentations that you can view anytime, some use a remote classroom that you dial into at lecture time, and some just use written or audio-recorded material. No matter what the format, the study methods described in this book will still be useful. With online courses that are not real-time, you have the advantage of being able to play back a passage of text or a video or audio segment if you didn't understand it. The disadvantage is that you can't ask questions until the professor has online office hours or checks his/her e-mail, so the amount of interpersonal interaction is usually less than in a regular course. Make a list of questions and ask them when your professor has office hours. You'll have to make adjustments to overcome the lack of in-person contact with the professor, but you should still take good notes, stay on top of the material, avoid distractions, allow enough time in your schedule for the course, and complete the assignments on time.

Hardships

Sometimes students have situations arise in their personal lives that intrude on their ability to study or perform well in a class. Problems ranging from a death in the family, an unexpected pregnancy, the break-up of a relationship, or a sudden move to a new location farther away from school (for commuter students) can drastically impact a student's performance. Sometimes students are reluctant to seek out help at school because they feel uncomfortable telling a stranger about a family problem. If the problem is affecting your ability to complete the work for the course, you really should speak to the professor or a counselor at the school as soon as you become aware that you might not be able to meet the requirements for the course. Sometimes dropping the course is the best thing to do. Most schools have deadlines during the semester for official withdrawal from a class. If you miss that deadline, you might end up with an unofficial withdrawal or administrative "F" on your transcript. If you are having a problem at home, please tell someone as early as possible so that you can get advice on how to handle your course load in light of this problem. If you wait too long, your options on how to deal with the problem

72

without affecting your academic record will be severely limited. There are counselors on campus who have a lot of experience in helping students cope with unexpected hardships at home. Many young people facing these types of problems feel that they are alone and that no one will understand, and this is natural, but it is not true. There are people who can help you, so don't try to shoulder the burden all by yourself!

Chapter 13

Attitude, Purpose, and Organization

▶▶▶▶▶▶▶▶▶▶▶▶▶▶▶▶▶▶▶▶▶▶▶▶▶▶▶▶▶▶▶▶▶▶▶▶▶▶▶

There are many things that go into a successful college experience. Hard work and discipline are two of the obvious ones, but having a positive attitude and a serious sense of purpose are also very important. As a college-bound freshman, you are most likely living away from home for the first time in your life and being expected to behave like an adult for the first time as well. Unlike when you were in high school, no one is going to follow you around in college making sure that you are doing what you are supposed to be doing. You, and you alone, have to make sure that things are getting done on time and getting done right. If you miss a class, your professor is not going to chase after you to make sure you know what you missed. It is your responsibility to find this out on your own. If you miss a due date or did not know what was going to be covered on an exam, you cannot just throw up your hands and say "I didn't know." This might have worked when you were kid, but those days are now over. Do yourself a favor, and start college with the attitude that you are personally responsible for your performance and the grades that you receive. If you run into trouble, adapt and make corrections in your behavior. Don't look for other people to blame! If you get a bad grade in a course, your professor did not "give you" a bad grade-you earned the bad grade yourself. One of the most important parts of becoming an adult is learning to accept personal responsibility; the buck stops here!

A positive attitude can also make life a lot easier and a lot more pleasant in college (and everywhere else, actually). You might occasionally have to take a course that you are not interested in order to satisfy the requirements for your major. Try looking at it this way: college is not just about learning facts and being trained for a career. It is about learning how to think critically and how to analyze. It is about learning how to solve problems that you have never seen before. These are skills that you can work on no matter what subject you are studying. If you are taking a class in which the material does not interest you, use it as an opportunity to improve your thinking, analytical, and/or writing skills. There is something useful that you can gain from any course, so find a way to make that course useful to you. If you are being required to take it, there must be a reason. Get what you can out of it!

Another, albeit less practical, way to look at it is that there is joy in learning just for the sake of learning. If you think you are not interested in this subject that you must study, try to keep an open mind and try to find something in it that does interest you. The professor probably has some enthusiasm for the subject, since it is an area of his/her expertise; try to pick up on that enthusiasm and try to share it. This may sound hokey, but it is better than sitting in a course being miserable!

You should also have a positive attitude about your workload. Remember, your college experience is totally for you and no one else. Everything they "make" you do in college is to foster your personal growth. The government is not forcing you to be there, and no one else should be forcing you to be there. What you learn or don't learn, what you take away from the college experience, is totally up to you. This is about your life, your career, and your success. This is about your learning how to think and become a productive person who can contribute something useful to the world. If you take a course and do the bare minimum amount of work needed just to get by, you are not "getting away with something." You are cheating yourself because you are not learning the subject matter. This affects no one but you! So, while you have this wonderful opportunity to learn all sorts of diverse things, use it to the fullest. Learn all you can, not just for the grades, but for yourself. It will make you better at whatever you end up doing with your life.

Another part of having a good attitude is being well-organized and punctual. Prepare properly for class or lab before you get there; think of the equipment you will need and make sure the equipment you have is in working order. If a procedure needs to be read ahead of time, do it; don't waste lab time reading material that you were supposed to read at home. If you are supposed to read something for lecture, read it before the lecture, not during! Listen to the professors when they tell you how to prepare for class, or what to bring to an exam. I can't even count how many times I've had students show up for a physics exam without a calculator, or who have written the exam in pencil after I announced four times that I wanted it written in ink. Before class, make sure you have enough paper, that your calculator batteries aren't dead, and that you have the right books with you. Also, don't keep asking the professor to repeat information that has already been given out. Keep your syllabus handy, keep a page where you list assignments and due dates, and don't lose it. Keep a folder for each class and put all your loose papers for that class in there, or punch them and put them in a binder. I recommend a loose-leaf binder with pockets for each course; that way you can add as much paper to it as you need but you won't be wasting unused paper at the end, like in a spiral notebook. Keep all of your old homeworks, lab reports, and exams; look over them before the final. When the course is over, don't throw everything out. Courses sometimes build on each other and the material you accumulate in one course might be useful in another.

You should do whatever you can to minimize the amount of stress in your life. This takes planning and effort—it doesn't just happen! A great way to minimize stress is to keep on top of your workload and don't let everything go until the last minute. If your schedule is constantly dictated by what has to be done absolutely right now, you'll be stressed out all of the time and the quality of your work won't be at its best. If you put some thought into time management and get assignments done *as they are given* rather than as they become due, you'll find that you have even more time to get things done and you'll feel better about everything. This then trickles down and affects everything in your life. Of course, it is also important to have the proper balance in your life, between school, work, other responsibilities, and fun. Too much or too little of any of these can throw everything out of balance, so start by making sure you have the appropriate credit load and that if you have a job you are not working too many hours during the semester. If you are having trouble deciding how to balance things out, talk to someone; there are academic counselors on campus who can help you to figure this out. Also be sure to get enough sleep; sleep deprivation is definitely not conducive to learning and being stress-free.

Being punctual is a really good habit to get into at any age, and the younger you are, the easier it is to start. Come to class on time. Most professors make announcements and give out assignments and other important information at the beginning of the class. If you walk in even five minutes late you will miss something, and it takes a lot more energy to find out what you missed than it does to get there on time, so just discipline yourself to arrive on time. It will soon be a habit that you won't even need to think about. Turn your assignments in on time, every time. Letting them pile up for weeks will not help you learn from the assignments, and that is what they are there for! Nothing ever gets done better when it is put off until the last minute, and it is certainly not easier and less stressful to do things this way. There is therefore no reason to procrastinate! It impresses no one, it doesn't improve your grade, and all it can do is create problems. You should also not wait until the night before something is due to *start* working on it. What if you get sick? What if your car breaks down? Now you'll have to either lose points for lateness, do a really bad rushed job, or ask your professor for an extension, when you really should have gotten it done sooner. Allow time for things to go wrong! Work is much easier and learning is more complete when it is done a little at a time, and if you keep to the schedule your professor sets for due dates, you will benefit. I know I keep harping on this idea of not putting things off, but that is because this is the number one thing I see people *not* doing that could help them change the most, for the better, if they would just do it. And, when you do enter the workforce as a professional, your employer will appreciate diligence, self-discipline, and punctuality— this is the stuff raises, job security, and promotions are made of! Good luck.

How to Study for Success in Science, Math, and Engineering Courses

by

Amy E. Bieber, Ph.D.

The author is a physics professor and the Director of the Laser and Fiber Optics Technology Program at The City University of New York, Queensborough Community College. She also teaches physics part-time at Hofstra University. She has worked in the aerospace, laser, semi-conductor, and intellectual property industries. She has just completed an A.A.S degree in Music Electronic Technology at Queensborough Community College, where she had a 4.0 average and was inducted into Phi Theta Kappa National Honor Society. She has a B.S. in Electrical Engineering from The Johns Hopkins University, where she graduated with full honors, was inducted into Eta Kappa Nu, the National Electrical Engineering Honor Society, and was an engineering scholarship recipient. The author has a Ph.D in Optics from the Institute of Optics at The University of Rochester, where she was a National Science Foundation Graduate Fellowship recipient.